POEMS
TO GROW ON

Poetry Activities for Young Children

by Mabel Chandler Duch

Fearon Teacher Aids
A Division of Frank Schaffer Publications, Inc.

W9-BEQ-055

This book is dedicated to
Charlene Duch Allen,
Denise Duch Edwards,
Eric Edwards,
and all the children who have shared
their worlds with me.

Senior Editor: Kristin Eclov
Editor: Cindy Barden
Cover Illustration: Rose Sheifer
Interior Illustration: Pauline Phung
Cover and Interior Design: Rose Sheifer Graphic Productions

© **Fearon Teacher Aids**
A Division of Frank Schaffer Publications, Inc.
23740 Hawthorne Boulevard
Torrance, CA 90505-5927

This Fearon Teachers Aids product was formerly manufactured and distributed by American Teaching Aids, Inc., a subsidiary of Silver Burdett Ginn, and is now manufactured and distributed by Frank Schaffer Publications, Inc. FEARON, FEARON TEACHERS AIDS, and the FEARON balloon logo are marks used under license from Simon & Shuster, Inc.

FE7949   ISBN 1-56417-949-4

Table of Contents

Introduction

A child's world is a marvelous place of wonder, imagination, and exploration. The poems in *Poems to Grow On* are written in the first person, from a child's point of view.

Some poems are about the child's self, others about the world of nature. They highlight childhood experiences and, along with the discussions and activities, stimulate imagination, verbal expression, and creativity.

As you read these poems to your students, you'll find they have favorites they want to hear over and over again. Indulge them by re-reading the ones they like best. Encourage children to memorize poems they enjoy. Make copies of the poems for the children to follow along as you read out loud to help improve their reading skills. After reading the poems, invite children to color the illustrations, and add drawings of their own.

The discussion section after each poem is designed to stimulate creative thinking and imagination. The related curriculum activities include arts and crafts projects, science, language arts, circle time activities, songs, and games.

Encourage children to make up their own poems. Ask classroom helpers or older students to write or type them. Have children decorate their poems and share them with the class.

Keep copies of children's poems. At the end of the school year, make a "best of" collection of poems. Be sure to include several poems from each student. Arrange them in a book by subject and make copies for students to take home and share with their families.

Other poetry books for children:

Sing a Song of Popcorn: Every Child's Book of Poems by Bernice De Regniers ed. (Scholastic, 1988)

Surprises and *More Surprises* by Lee Bennett Hopkins (Harper, 1984 and 1987)

The Random House Book of Poetry for Children (Random House, 1983)

Where the Sidewalk Ends by Shel Silverstein (Harper & Row, 1974)

Now That I am Big

When I was very, very small,
I couldn't walk or talk at all.
But now that I am big, almost–
('Tho Mother says I shouldn't boast–)
I can talk and I can shout!
I can walk and run about
Faster than my father can
'Tho I'm a boy and he's a man.
I can dance and I can sing;
I can do most anything.
I'm glad I am no longer small;
That wasn't any fun at all.

- What are skills? Name some skills. Remind children that not all skills are physical. Reading and counting, for example, are also skills.

- What is your earliest memory? What can you do now that you couldn't do when you were younger?

- Can you remember learning a new skill? What was it? How did you feel?

- Do you have a younger brother or sister? What can you do that he or she can't?

- Have you ever watched a young child learning a new skill? What was it? What did the child do or say when he or she mastered it?

- Ask your parents about how you learned a new skill when you were younger, such as walking or talking.

The Way We Were—Look at Us Now

Have children bring in photos of themselves when they were younger. Encourage them to bring in pictures of themselves learning new skills like walking, bicycle or tricycle riding. Have children bring in pictures of themselves doing new activities, too. Then create "The Way We Were" and "Look at Us Now!" bulletin boards.

Take pictures of children learning new skills in the classroom to add to the display.

Group Poem

Write the words "Now that I am big, I can . . . ." on a chalkboard or on chart paper. Ask children to take turns finishing the sentence. For example, "Now that I am big, I can ride my bike without training wheels" or "Now that I am big, I can stay up later at night." Record the children's responses on the chalkboard. Then have the children copy the sentences in their writing journals.

Circle Time

Divide the class into small groups. Ask children in each group to take turns demonstrating a skill they have learned without using any words. Invite the other group members to guess what skill is being demonstrated.

Super Hero Skills

Divide the class into small groups. Have them work together to make a super hero with super hero skills. Ask one child from each group to describe their group's super hero and his or her special skills.

Antonyms

The poem "Now That I am Big" compares what it was like when the child was small to how it is now that he or she is big. Explain that the words *big* and *small* are opposites. Words that are opposites are also called *antonyms*. Write a list of words on the chalkboard, such as *big, happy, quiet, short, thin,* and *work.* Help students name the antonyms for each word. Encourage the group to add to the list of antonyms.

Jobs I Can Do

As children grow, they are given more privileges and responsibilities at home and at school. Explain the meaning of the words *privileges* and *responsibilities.* (Privileges are the rights to do certain things, such as stay up later or watch television. Responsibilities are things that people expect to be done without asking, such as homework or chores.) Ask students to name some privileges and responsibilities they now have that they didn't have when they were younger.

Growth Charts

Have each child make a personal growth chart inside the cover of his or her writing journal. Attach a measuring tape to the wall for children to measure their heights throughout the year. Measure children at the beginning, in the middle, and at the end of the school year. Have them record their heights and the date they were measured on their personal growth charts.

If you have the equipment, take a photograph of each child at the beginning of the school year and again at the end. At the end of the year, send both photos home with the children to share with their families.

Growing Up: Related Books for Young Children

Someone New by Charlotte Zolotow (Harper, 1978)
Leo the Late Bloomer by Robert Kraus (Harper, 1971)
The Growing Story by Ruth Krauss (Harper, 1947)

Useful Things

Mouths are very useful things:
They eat and smile and talk.
Legs and feet are useful things:
They skip and run and walk.
Eyes are very useful things:
They cry and look and wink.
But our most useful body parts
Are arms and hands, I think.
Hands can work and hands can clap;
And arms can hold you tight.
Arms and hands will tuck you in
When you are tired at night.

Reproducible

Discussion

- What body parts were mentioned in the poem? (mouths, legs, feet, eyes, arms, and hands)
- How are mouths useful?
- How are legs and feet useful?
- How are eyes useful?
- How are arms and hands useful?
- There are two other body parts on your head. What are they? What do they do? (Your nose smells, breathes, and sneezes. Your ears hear, and maybe wiggle.)
- On the chalkboard, write the body parts mentioned in the poem. Ask children to name action words and write these words under the appropriate body parts.

Mouths	Legs and Feet	Eyes	Hands and Arms
eat	skip	cry	hug
drink	kick	wink	pat
smile	run	look	clap
frown	walk	read	draw

Other Useful Things

In the poem, "Useful Things" the poet writes about different parts of the body and how they are useful. Explain the meaning of the word *useful* (can be used for more than one purpose or helpful). Ask children to think of other things that are useful. Record the students' responses on a chalkboard or on chart paper. Encourage children to draw a picture of a useful object. Ask them to show their pictures to the class and explain why they think that object is useful.

Pantomime

The child in this poem thinks arms and hands are the most useful body parts. Ask the children what body part mentioned in the poem they think is the most useful?

Without speaking or pointing, can you show what part you think is the most useful? Use actions only. Acting without words is called *pantomiming*.

Have each child show a friend what body part he or she thinks is the most useful. Challenge children to guess what part was chosen.

Act It Out

Read the poem, "Useful Things" to the class. Ask them to act out the action words as you say them.

Looby Loo

Play the old time folk game "Looby Loo" with the children. After each verse, join hands and circle around while singing the refrain.

2. left hand
3. right foot
4. left foot
5. head right
6. whole self

Reproducible

My Pie

I made a pie like Mother's.
It's big and thick and round;
And such a pretty color:
A delicious chocolate brown.

You say you'd like a piece of it?
I'd share it if I could.
But I don't think you'd like it;
My pie is made of mud!

Reproducible

> Have you ever made a mud pie? Tell us about it.
> Of course, you would never eat a mud pie, would you? Why not? How about a leaf pie? A bug pie?
> What is your favorite kind of pie?
> Make up an imaginary pie, one that's good to eat.

Guess What Is In My Pie

Invite children to bring something from home that could be an ingredient in an imaginary pie, such as a teddy bear, a toy car, or a lollipop. Ask parents to send their child's object to school in a paper grocery bag. You will also need an empty pie tin. Explain to the children that the items are in bags so they can be kept a secret until after sharing time. Have children take turns placing their paper bags in the pie tin and giving one clue to the contents of the bag. Invite the other students to ask ten questions about the item. If the children can not guess the contents of the bag, the child with the bag can show the object and choose the next person.

Circle Time

Read the children's poems "Little Jack Horner" and "Sing a Song of Six Pence" to the class several times. Read each line of the poem and encourage children to act it out.

As a class, read the poems together and act them out.

Mud Pies

If you have cooking facilities, make an edible "Mud Pie" (chocolate pie). Invite the children to help with measuring and mixing. Use the recipe below.

Edible Mud Pie

1 cup (240 ml) sugar	3 egg yolks or 2 large eggs
1/4 cup (60 ml) cornstarch	2 cups (480 ml) milk
1/3 cup (80 ml) cocoa	1 teaspoon (5 ml) vanilla

Combine dry ingredients. Pour a small amount of milk in the top of a double boiler. Add dry ingredients to the milk and mix until smooth. Beat the eggs and then add them to the milk mixture, stirring well. Add the remaining milk and cook over hot water in the double boiler. Stir the mixture constantly until it becomes thick. Then cover the double boiler and cook another 10 minutes, stirring occasionally. Remove the mixture from the heat, add vanilla and cool. Pour into a graham cracker pie crust and chill.

When the pie is cold, serve with whipped cream or non-dairy whipped topping. This is one "mud" pie children will love!

On My Way to School Today

On my way to school today,
I saw a Flipposaur at play
It folded back its purple wings;
Did handstands, flips, and other things.
It rolled and tumbled on the ground;
Then off it flew without a sound.
I haven't told a soul but you,
'Cause others might not think it's true.

"On My Way to School Today" appeared in the September/October 1992 issue of Good Apple's magazine, *Lollipops* and is used with permission.

**Discussion**

- Have you ever imagined something that seemed so real you almost believed it were true? Can you give an example?
- What imaginary creature might you meet on the way to school? What would it look like? What would you name it? What would it do?

What I Might Have Seen

Invite children to draw an imaginary animal or creature and show it in action, if possible. Encourage them not to show their drawings to anyone.

When the drawings are finished, ask children to pair off. Have them take turns describing their drawings without showing their pictures to their partners. As one child describes his or her creature, have the other child draw it.

When they finish, have the children compare their drawings to the originals.

Mulberry Street

Read the book *And to Think that I Saw it on Mulberry Street* by Dr. Seuss (Random, 1989) to the class. Ask the children to name ways this story is like the poem "On My Way to School Today."

Another Imaginary Creature

Divide children into groups of five or six. Give each group a large piece of paper and crayons. Ask one child to draw and color the head of an imaginary animal. Pass the drawing to other members of the group, and have each one add other parts to the drawing—body, legs, tail, wings, ears, trunk, scales, fins, wheels, etc.

Ask the group to decide on a name for the creature when they finish. Write the creature's name on the paper and display the drawings on the bulletin board as part of an imaginary zoo.

If You're Happy . . .

Sing the song "If You're Happy and You Know It" with the class. Instead of the usual verses, add new ones, like wink your eye, wave your hand, wiggle your nose. Invite children to suggest ideas for new verses.

Soap Bubble

Soap bubble, soap bubble,
Floating in the breeze,
Upward, upward,
Above the house and trees.

I wish that I were tiny;
I wish that I were small,
Small enough to fit inside
That shiny little ball.

The wind would rock me gently
As I am looking down
At bug-like people
In a little tiny town.

Bug-like people
Rushing here and there
As I am floating gently
In my bubble in the air.

Discussion

▶ If you could ride in a soap bubble, where would you go?

▶ Suppose you were in a bubble floating above your school. What would you see?

▶ What do you think happens to bubbles when they pop?

Blowing Bubbles

On a nice breezy day, take the children outside to blow soap bubbles. You can buy bubble kits or you can make your own.

Take a piece of thin wire about eight inches long (20 cm). Make a circle in one end—the size of a 50 cent piece. Tape over any sharp ends.

Make a bubble mixture of dish soap or detergent and water. Have children measure the water and then the soap. Encourage children to experiment to see what ratio works best for bubbles. Equal amounts of water and soap work well.

Dip a wire circle into the bubble mixture until the opening is covered with film. Hold the wire circle near your mouth and gently blow.

Encourage children to take turns blowing bubbles. Have them measure how far some bubbles travel and time how long some bubbles last. Have fun!

Bubble Words

Draw a large bubble (circle) on the chalkboard. Ask children to name words that begin with the letter B and have two syllables. Give some examples, such as *baby, buggy, bunny,* and *banjo*. Write the words in the circle as children name them.

Alliteration

Write a sentence using "B" words on a chalkboard or on chart paper. For example, Barry's brother baked a batch of brownies. Have volunteers come up and underline all the "B" words used in the sentence. Ask children to take turns making up other sentences using as many "B" words as they can. Record the sentences on the chalkboard. Give each child a sheet of writing paper. Help children cut the paper into bubble shapes. Have children write their "B" sentences on their bubbles and then decorate them.

Bubble Ride

As a class, discuss what it would be like to travel in a bubble. Encourage children to write stories about their bubble adventures in their writing journals. Invite students to illustrate their stories and share them with the class.

Clouds

Over in the meadow,
There's a place where I
Like to sit beneath a tree
And watch the clouds drift by:
Thin wispy clouds
Stretched across the sky;
Thick, fluffy clouds
Piled up high.
When you look up at the clouds,
You can see most anything:
Cloud knights guard
A castle for the king;
Cloud cats prowl
On little cloud feet;
And cloud children play
On a cloud-lined street.
Cloud horses gallop;
And cloud birds fly,
When I sit beneath my tree
And watch the clouds drift by.

Discussion

▶ Have you ever looked for shapes in clouds? What did you see?

▶ What often happens when clouds are dark? (rain or snow)

Cloud Watching

On a day when the sky is filled with fluffy clouds, take the children outside. Ask them to look for shapes of objects in the clouds. As the clouds change encourage children to look for new shapes. Share the book *Hi, Clouds* by Carol Green (Childrens, 1983).

Cloud Art

Invite children to make cloud pictures. Have them glue cotton balls into cloud shapes on 9" x 12" (22.5 cm x 30 cm) light blue construction paper. Encourage children to draw or cut out birds, butterflies, and bees and add them to their pictures. If possible, display the pictures on the ceiling to create a sky full of clouds.

Cloud Study

Provide books about clouds for the children to enjoy. Share the book *The Cloud Book* by Tomie dePaola (Holiday House, 1975). Use the Cloud Facts section to teach children about the different types of clouds—*cirrus, cirrostratus, cumulus, stratocumulus, stratus, cumulonimbus,* altostratus, altocumulus, and *cirrocumulus.*

Cloud Facts:

What is a cloud? A cloud is a collection of water droplets or ice crystals formed when moisture (water vapor) condenses around tiny dust, smoke, or salt particles in the air. (Condensation can be demonstrated by holding a spoon above a steaming kettle.)

Why are clouds white? Sunshine reflects off the water droplets or ice crystals in the clouds, making them appear white.

Why do some clouds look dark? When there is much moisture in clouds, the droplets make shadows and the clouds appear dark.

Give children a copy of the next page with the pictures of different types of clouds. Then give them the following information:

▶ Delicate wispy or curly clouds high in the sky are called *cirrus* after "cirro" meaning curl.

▶ Thick, fluffy, piled-up clouds are called *cumulus.*

▶ Blanket-like, usually low clouds are called *stratus.*

Names are combined to describe some clouds. *Nimbus* or *nimbo* added to a cloud's name often means it is a rain or snow cloud. Go outside and help children identify the different types of clouds by name.

Clouds

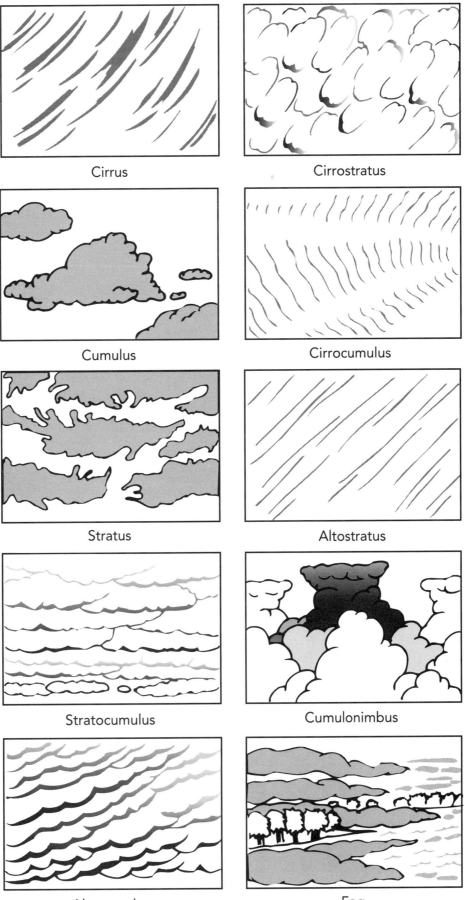

Cirrus

Cirrostratus

Cumulus

Cirrocumulus

Stratus

Altostratus

Stratocumulus

Cumulonimbus

Altocumulus

Fog

　　　　Reproducible

Fog

I like fog—it's mystery
You never know what you might see.
What might appear quite suddenly
From out of the mist.

You never know just what's in store:
A dragon or a dinosaur;
A giant or a mighty king.
It might be almost anything
From out of the mist.

Reproducible

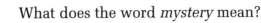

Discussion

▶ What does the word *mystery* mean?

▶ What do you think might be hidden in the fog?

▶ What would you do if something suddenly appeared in the fog?

▶ What delightful thing would you like to find in the fog?

▶ How are fog and clouds alike?

Foggy Pictures

Have children draw pictures of what they think might be in the fog. Cover pictures with one or two thin sheets of tissue paper to give a fog-like effect.

Fog Facts:

Explain these fog facts to the class.

▶ What is fog? (Fog is a cloud on or near the earth's surface.)

▶ What makes fog? (Fog is formed by warm, moist air passing over cold water or land. Sometimes it is formed when warm and cold air meet or when cold air passes over warm water.)

▶ How can fog be a problem? (It's hard to see in fog, which can cause traffic problems. Fog combined with smoke or auto exhaust makes smog which causes breathing problems in some people.)

▶ How is fog helpful? (It provides moisture for plants, helping to keep them green. It also helps animals hide from predators.)

Fog Books:

Fog in the Meadow by Joanne Ryder (Harper & Row, 1979)
Hide and Seek Fog by Alvin Tresselt (Lothrop, Lee & Shepard Co., 1965)

What Rhymes with Fog?

Write the letters "og" on the chalkboard ten times. Encourage children to make ten new words that rhyme with the word *fog—bog, dog, frog, hog, clog, log, jog, polliwog, groundhog,* and *catalog.* Show children how to change the letters to make the new rhyming words.

Take a Vote

As a class, discuss what fog looks like. For those children who have not experienced it, explain what fog look likes. Then ask the class to vote on the question "Do you like fog?" Divide the children into two groups, based on their answers. Ask them to take turns giving a reason why they do or do not like fog.

Foggy Adjectives

Ask children to name as many words as they can that describe the word *fog*. Record the children's responses on the chalkboard—*gray, misty, creepy, silent, fuzzy, eerie*, and so on.

Follow the Foghorn

A foghorn helps guide ships to safety when it is too foggy to see where they are going. The captain of the ship listens to the foghorn to find his or her way. Invite children to take turns being a foghorn or a ship. Play this game in a gym or in a room without obstacles.

Blindfold the child who is the ship and spin him or her around several times. Have the child who is the foghorn stand across the room and make sounds to guide the "ship" to shore. When the ship touches the child playing the foghorn the ship has safely arrived on shore.

Circle Time Story

As a class, make up an oral group story about a foggy day. Use one of the story starters provided or one of your own. Have each child take a turn adding a few sentences to continue the story. Continue until everyone has had a chance to contribute. Ask the last child to make up an ending.

1. My family and I went on a camping trip. We slept in a tent in the woods. I woke up before anyone else and looked outside. It was dark and foggy. Suddenly, out of the fog, I saw . . .

2. One dark November night, I couldn't sleep. I looked out my bedroom window. It was so foggy outside I couldn't see the house across the street. Suddenly, out of the fog, I saw . . .

"Fog" by Carl Sandburg

Read the poem "Fog" by Carl Sandburg (found in *The Random House Book of Poetry for Children*, Random House, 1983). Have children listen closely as you read the words. As a class, talk about Sandburg's description of the fog. Invite children to draw a picture to illustrate the poem. If interested, encourage children to write their own poems about fog.

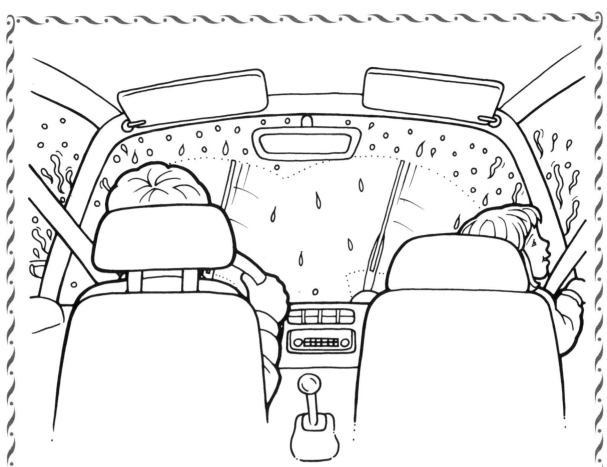

Rainy Ride

It's snug and dry within the car,
But wild and wet outside,
Though some complain and some may whine,
I like a rainy ride.
I like to hear the raindrops
Beating on the glass.
I like to watch the giant trucks
Splush-splashing as they pass.
I like to see the wipers
Swinging to and fro;
And watch the wriggling raindrops
As up the panes they go.
Riding through a rainstorm
It's great to be alive!
But Daddy says I feel that way
'Cause I don't have to drive.

Reproducible

> Have you ever noticed that raindrops on the window of a moving car go up. Do you know why? (They are pushed up by the wind created by the car's motion.)

> Why does the child in the poem like a rainy ride?

> How does her father feel about driving in the rain? (He doesn't like it.) Can you think of why? (Driving in the rain can be dangerous because it is more difficult to see and the road may be slippery. Dad will have to drive more slowly than usual and be very attentive to road conditions and traffic.)

Imaginary Hide and Seek

(A game for two or more players.)

Pretend you are very tiny. Choose a make-believe hiding place. This can be inside the car behind the sun visor or outside the car in a stoplight.

Players guess where you are hiding by asking questions you answer with "Yes" or "No." For example; "Is it in the car?" See how many questions it takes to reveal your hiding place. Limit the number of questions to 21 or less. The player who correctly guesses your hiding place gets a turn to "hide."

I See

This is a memory game based on what players observe out the car's windows. First player mentions something he or she sees. For example, "I see an old farm house." Second player repeats what first player said and adds two of something he or she sees. For example, "I see an old farm house and two tall trees."

Next player repeats the entire sentence and adds three of something he or she has seen. ("I see an old farm house, two tall trees, and three fat cows.") The game continues until a player can't remember the entire sentence. Last player to repeat the sentence correctly and add his or her number of objects, wins.

Scenes Through a Car Window

Cut 12" x 18" (30 cm x 45 cm) black paper frames in the shape of car windows. Give children 12" x 18" (30 cm x 45 cm) art paper and have them draw a scene they've seen through a car window, such as a city block or a field with cows. Frame the pictures using the car-window frames. Display the car-window scenes on a wall or bulletin board.

Rainy Sounds

After reading the poem "Rainy Ride," ask the children to recall sound words from the poem. Encourage them to describe other sounds made by the rain as well as the sounds made by people walking and vehicles driving in the rain.

My Tree

Over by the meadow
Is the tree that I like best.
It's straight and strong and smooth-barked,
And taller than the rest.
This tree is great for climbing,
And if you climb up high
And stretch your arms, you almost can,
Almost touch the sky.

 **Discussion**

- Do you have a favorite tree? What makes it your favorite?
- Can you name different types of trees?
- Why are trees important? (They provide shade, shelter, home for birds and animals, and keep the soil from eroding.)
- What do we get from trees? (Wood, fruit, nuts, flowers, acorns, pinecones.)

Tree Study

After reading the poem "My Tree" invite children to draw pictures of trees. Display the tree pictures on the wall. Then take the children outside to see trees firsthand. Encourage them to observe trees from a distance and close up. Have them feel the bark and leaves from different trees and then look up and see the branches, too.

After returning to the classroom, have the children draw pictures of trees again. When they are finished drawing, display the new pictures on the wall, too. Encourage the children to compare the trees. Do they look different? Why?

Imaginary Trees

What if money grew on trees? Or, chocolate chip cookies? Or, new shoes? Ask children what kind of an imaginary tree they would like to have growing in their yards. Invite them to describe their imaginary trees and then draw pictures of them.

Tree ID

Have children gather fallen leaves, acorns, nuts, and pinecones from different types of trees. Provide tree identification reference books. Help children identify the type of trees their leaves, acorns, and nuts came from. Glue the leaves, nuts, acorns, and pinecones to paper and write the names of the trees they came from.

Make a Poet-tree

Find a bare tree branch about three feet (90 cm) long with lots of smaller branches. Place the branch in a pail or large coffee can and anchor the branch with sand or gravel. Cut out large paper leaves from colored construction paper. Invite each child to write a short poem about trees on a paper leaf and then write his or her name on the back. Attach the leaves to the "poet-tree" with thread or paper clips.

Bird Song

There's a bird who sings to me.
He's sitting by my window in a tree.
He sings the same song everyday.
I wish I knew what he wants to say.

Reproducible

Discussion

▶ Nearly all birds call and about half of them call and sing. A *birdcall* is only one sound, which may be repeated. A *song* is a series of notes arranged in a pattern. Why do birds call? (Baby birds call to tell their mothers and sometimes their fathers when they are hungry. Adult birds call to other birds usually to alert others of danger.)

▶ Usually only male birds sing. Why do they sing? (To attract a mate and to tell other birds "This is my territory. Stay out.")

Bird Sounds

Using tapes, teach children to recognize birdcalls and songs. Birds with calls or songs easy to recognize are—Blue Jay, Bob-link, Bobwhite, Crow, Loon, and Mourning Dove.

Recommended Audio Tapes

Common Bird Songs (Animal Town, Santa Barbara, CA 93120)
Songs of Eastern Birds (Animal Town, Santa Barbara, CA 93120)
Songs of Western Birds (Animal Town, Santa Barbara, CA 93120)
Field Guide to Bird Songs (Houghton Mifflin)

Bird Study

The best way to study birds is by direct observation. If you are willing to commit to a continuous feeding program, you can make bird feeders to attract birds to your classroom window. If you are feeding the birds, you need to also provide water.

Simple Bird Feeders

Place suet in a mesh bag and hang it outside your window. Apples (with a section of skin removed), cranberries, unshelled peanuts, and meaty bones can be tied to tree branches near your classroom to attract birds, too.

Aluminum muffin or pie tins also make good bird feeders. Make small drainage holes in the tins with a nail and hammer. Fill the tins with bird seed, bread crumbs, or fruit.

Pinecone Feeders

Show students how to make pinecone feeders. Mix smooth peanut butter with an equal amount of corn meal. Have children spread the mixture on the pinecones using craft sticks. Tie a loop of yarn to the pinecone as a hanger. Place the finished pinecone feeders in plastic sandwich bags for children to take home.

The Good Old Days

Grandma says, when she was small,
They didn't have TV at all—
Nor even one computer game.
But they "were happy, all the same,"
With puzzles, books and radio
And outdoor games I'll never know.

I think that they were very brave:
They cooked without a microwave.
And Grandpa said they had a rule
That children had to walk to school.
I'm glad that I'm a child today
And never had to live that way.

Discussion

▶ According to the poem, what things do we have now that Grandma and Grandpa couldn't enjoy when they were children? (TV, computer games, computers, microwaves, and school buses) Which of these things would you miss most if you couldn't use them?

▶ What did people in the past do for entertainment? (Puzzles, books, radio, outdoor games) Which of these pastimes do you still enjoy today?

▶ Here are some games your grandparents played. Which of them do you play?

Follow the Leader	Leap Frog
Green Light, Red Light	Tag
Hide and Go Seek	Hopscotch
Paper, Scissors, Rock	Marbles
Jacks	Mother, May I
Jump Rope	Pom-Pom Pullaway

Old Time Radio

Before TV, people enjoyed comedies and dramas on radio, which allowed them to use their imaginations. Audio cassettes of these programs are available from many sources, including public libraries.

Your children might enjoy listening to *The Cinnamon Bear* stories, available from Radio Spirits, Inc.; P.O. Box 2141; Schiller Park, IL 60176.

Invite Guests

Invite grandparents, great-grandparents and perhaps some senior citizens to come in and share pre-TV activities with your children. These could include stories, simple jigsaw puzzles, simple card games, checkers, and outdoor games the children may not know. Encourage children to ask their guests to describe "the good old days."

About the Good Old Days

Encourage children to finish one of these sentences:
"I'm glad I didn't live in the good old days because . . ."
"I wish I had lived in the good old days because . . ."

Have classroom helpers or older students help children write or dictate the completed sentences on pieces of construction paper. Ask children to draw pictures about the sentences they wrote.

Old-Fashioned Rag Dolls

Long ago children played with homemade toys, like rag or corn-husk dolls, wooden wagons, and hoops. Invite the children to make their own homemade rag dolls.

Rag dolls and animals were made from material left over from sewing projects or clothes too old to repair. Provide a variety of colors and textures of fabric to make rag dolls or animal shapes. A local thrift shop could be a good source of fabric. Help children cut or tear the material into strips. Twist the material into shapes for arms, legs, a body, and a head. Attach the body parts with string, thread, or rubber bands. Invite the children to decorate the faces of their rag dolls with paint or markers. Help children braid yarn or string for hair or animal tails.

Old-Fashioned Games

Before television, children played all sorts of games. Teach your class to play the games Marbles, Leapfrog, Hopscotch, or Paper, Scissors, Rock. Checkers was another favorite game. Gather or make several checker boards and hold a checkers championship. Encourage the children to spend their spare time in class playing old-fashioned games.

Books About The Good Old Days for Young Children

Encourage students to read more about this country's history. Provide a variety of library books for children to enjoy.

The Story of a Main Street by John S. Goodall (Macmillan, 1987)

Ox-Cart Man by Donald Hall (Viking, 1979)

My Prairie Year: Based on the Dairy of Elenore Plaisted by Brett Harvey (Holiday, 1986)

A Birthday for Blue by Kerry Raines Lydon (Whitman, 1989)

The Cornhusk Doll by Evelyn Minshull (Herald Press, 1987)

Dakota Dugout by Ann Turner (Macmillan, 1985)

Careers

Jenny says a doctor
Is what she wants to be.
Mark would be a lawyer,
And Kay would go to sea.

I'd like to be a pizza man
And make the children smile.
I'd toss my dough up in the air,
Singing all the while.

I'd make a million pizzas,
As many as I could.
And I would give free pizzas
To everyone who's good.

Reproducible

- Why does the child in the poem want to be a pizza maker?

- What is your favorite kind of pizza? What toppings do you like? Sliced bananas? Chocolate chips? Marshmallows and whipped cream? Peanut butter and jelly? What toppings would you add if you could make up your very own special pizza?

- What do you want to be when you grow up? Why?

- Kay from the poem says she wants to go to sea. What could her occupation be? (She could join the navy, work on a research ship, or on a fishing boat.)

- What other occupations are mentioned in the poem? (doctor, lawyer)

Careers in Action

- Visit a pizza parlor where you can see the pizzas being made.

- Visit some places where careers are practiced. (Suggestions: fire station, bank, city hall, newspaper, retail shops, farms)

- Some parents may be willing to come in to explain their occupations to the children. Plan ahead of time to have interested parents come in for brief presentations about their occupations. Encourage children to ask questions.

Being a Teacher

Tell the children about yourself.
- Why did you choose to be a teacher?
- How old were you when you decided?
- How did you prepare to be a teacher?
- What do you like about teaching?
- What responsibilities and challenges do you have?

Careers Collage

Have children cut out pictures from old magazines of people doing various jobs. Working in groups, children can glue the pictures to large pieces of construction paper to make a careers collage.

Today's Jobs

Today people work as computer operators, taxi, truck, and bus drivers, pilots, and electricians. Ask children to name other jobs that didn't exist 100 years ago and explain why not.

Jobs That Have Changed

Some jobs like farmers, doctors, bankers, bakers, and school teachers existed 100 years ago but the tools they used to do their jobs were very different. Ask students to name a variety of different tools. Record their responses on the chalkboard. As a class, discuss how tools have changed. Encourage the children to name tools that have not changed, such as a rolling pin, a shovel, a wheel barrow, and so on.

Someday...

Ask children to name different jobs adults do. Record children's ideas on the board. Have them think about the type of job they would like to do when they grow up. What skills will they need to learn to do that job? How will they learn those skills? Ask children to draw pictures of themselves as adults doing that job.

Career Box

Fill a box with a variety of items or pictures of items people might use to do their jobs, such as a pencil, stethoscope, hammer, pliers, duct tape, small shovel, spool of thread, computer disk, toy truck, paintbrush, and so on. Give one object or picture to each child. Invite each child to name the object and the type of job it could be used for. Record the children's responses on the chalkboard or on chart paper. Ask the class for other ideas about different jobs that might use the same object. For example, a pencil might be used by a teacher, a banker, a doctor, a writer, an architect, or an artist.

Dress-Up Day

Ask children to bring or wear something that represents a type of job adults do. For example, a stethoscope, a hard hat, a firefighter's hat, a uniform, and so on. Have children take turns naming the job they are dressed for and telling about it.

Fun Jobs

The person in the poem "Careers" would like to be a pizza maker. Ask children to think of other jobs that might be really fun to do, like balloon seller, dog walker, popcorn seller, sports professional, candy maker, and face painter. Invite children to make up short poems about fun jobs they would like to do.

My Teddy Bear

My Teddy Bear has lost an eye.
His fur is worn and shabby.
He has a rip upon his back
Where he was clawed by Tabby.
His leg is loose and wobbly.
His ear displays a tear.
I've other toys bright and new;
But I love my Teddy Bear!

 **Discussion**

- What is your favorite toy?
- How long have you had it?
- Would you ever consider throwing it away? Why or why not?

Sharing Toys

Encourage the children to bring in toys to share. Set up guidelines for the treatment of other children's toys.

Guidelines might include:

- Be sure your hands are clean before touching a toy.
- Do not take a toy without permission of the owner or without sharing your toy.
- Do not keep a toy beyond agreed time limit.
- Be gentle with the toy. Do not squash, throw, or drop it.

Encourage a discussion or writing time about the toy sharing experience. Suggested questions:

- Did you get to play with a toy you have never seen before?
- What did you like about this toy?
- Did you have any problems during sharing time? How did you solve them?
- Are you happy to have your own toy back?

Guess What It Is?

Ask children to bring a favorite toy to school in a paper bag stapled or taped shut. On the outside of the bag, ask children (with parents' help) to write three clues about the toy inside. Clues can include the material it is made of, the color, the overall shape, or the sound it makes.

Encourage children to take turns reading their clues to the class. Classmates can ask additional questions that can be answered with a "yes" or "no" until children guess correctly. When the mystery toy is correctly identified, the child can then show it to the class.

My Poem

Encourage children to make up a poem about a favorite toy. Remind them that the poem doesn't have to rhyme. Have classroom helpers or older students record the poems. Invite children to add drawings of their favorite toys to their poems.

Compare and Contrast

Divide the class into small groups. Select two of the children's stuffed animals from each group. Ask the children to name ways the two toys are alike. Then ask them to think of ways the two are different. Encourage the children to use size, color, texture, eye color, and number of legs to compare and contrast the stuffed animals.

Grouping

Gather the children's stuffed animals together. Ask children to sort them by different characteristics, such as color, size, wild or domestic animals, eye color, whether they have tails or not, and so on. Encourage children to discuss the criteria they used to sort the animals. Then invite children to arrange all the animals by size from smallest to largest.

What is it?

Invite volunteers to take turns being blindfolded. Give the blindfolded child one stuffed animal to hold. Then ask him or her to feel the shape of the animal and guess what it is.

Pet Show

Ask children to bring an unusual stuffed animal to class. If someone doesn't have a stuffed animal, a plastic one would do, too. Have children display their toys for all to enjoy.

Make up enough blue ribbon awards or certificates for all the children. You can leave the category blank until it's time for the judging. Award blue ribbons to animals in different categories. You may need to be creative to come up with a blue ribbon for every child. Categories might include *softest, bluest, fuzziest, largest, smallest, silliest, happiest, most legs, longest tail, longest ears, pinkest, most stripes,* or *most spots.*

Islands

Do you have a favorite island,
A little piece of ground
In the middle of a lake or stream
With water all around?

Or better yet an island
In some far southern seas,
Like the little island
Unknown to all but me.

There are flowers on my island
And giant stingless bees, Rainbow-colored birds
And slender, curling trees.

There's a castle on my island
And a buried treasure chest.
All these things are wonderful,
But here's what I like best:
There's room upon my island
For a special friend or two;
And if you don't have an island,
I'll share my one with you.

Reproducible

> **Discussion**

▶ What is an island? (A piece of land completely surrounded by water)

▶ The owner of the island says no one else knows about it. But other people have been on the island. How do we know? (The castle and the buried treasure. It's unlikely the owner could have built the castle and buried the treasure alone.)

▶ Do you think the island is real or make believe? Why do you think so?

▶ If you owned an island, what would you want on it? Who would you invite to visit?

My Island

Divide the class into small groups. Invite each group to make three dimensional maps of their imaginary islands. Have each group mix 2 cups (480 ml) flour, 1 cup (240 ml) salt, and 1/4 cup (60 ml) water to make clay.

Have each group use their clay to mold an island on a stiff piece of cardboard. Paint the ocean around the island blue. Show children how to make indentations in their islands to form rivers, lakes, volcanoes, hills, and valleys. When the children have finished, set the islands aside to dry.

Then have each group decorate their islands with tempera paint. Encourage children to make buildings, trees, and animals to add to their islands.

On My Island

Provide a small throw rug or carpet square for each child. Ask children to place their "islands" in the sea (the floor of the classroom or gym.) When children are sitting on their islands, have them play the game "I See" (for directions see page 26).

Island Collage

Have children cut out an island-shape (a large irregular shape) from any color of construction paper. Provide old magazines for children to cut out pictures of objects and animals they would like to have living on their islands. Glue the pictures to the paper to make an island collage. Display the collages in the classroom.

Treasure Chests

Have children make their own treasure chests from cardboard shoeboxes.

To decorate, use aluminum foil, wrapping paper, wall paper, glitter, glue, rick rack, and other craft items. Invite children to use their treasure chests to store their own favorite treasures or collections of small objects.

Boxes Big and Small

With boxes, boxes, boxes,
Boxes big and small,
I can be and I can do
Anything at all.

I can build a castle
And be a mighty king.
I can build myself a stage
And act and dance and sing.

I can make a cavern
With giant bats inside,
A deep and dark mysterious place
Where dragons like to hide.

I can fight the dragons
To set a princess free.
With my imagination,
I can always be
Anything I want, anything at all,
With the help of boxes,
Boxes big and small.

Reproducible

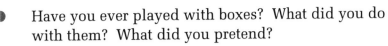

▶ Have you ever played with boxes? What did you do with them? What did you pretend?

▶ What did the child in the poem build with boxes? (castle, stage, cavern)

▶ What did the child pretend to be? (a king)

▶ What did the child do? (act, dance, sing, and free a princess from a dragon)

Boxes Big and Small

Bring in a collection of boxes varying in size from small to very big. (Parents could be asked to contribute boxes.) Invite children to engage in creative play with the boxes.

Have them dictate or write stories about their box experiences. What did they pretend to be? What happened in their box adventures?

Encourage them to illustrate their stories, then tape them to the boxes which inspired their adventures.

Box Town

Bring in boxes of various sizes from very small (jewelry size) up to the size of a shoebox or cereal box. Food container boxes come in a variety of sizes and shapes. Provide children with colored paper, crayons, markers, scissors, and glue. Invite children to create buildings for a tabletop Box Town.

Children can cut out windows and make swinging doors. They can make sidewalks from long strips of white poster board. Use wider strips of black poster board for roads. Add small toy animals, cars, people, and trees to complete the town.

Box Cave

Encourage children to pile up large boxes to make a box cave. Have them cut out black paper bats to decorate the inside of the cave. Provide a flashlight for the cave explorers.

Music Boxes

Invite children to make great percussion instruments from empty boxes of different sizes and shapes. Unsharpened pencils are great for drumsticks or children can play with their hands like a bongo drum. To make shakers use small boxes partially filled with dried rice, cereal, marbles, or other small objects. Tightly tape the boxes shut. Play marching band music or other lively music. Invite children to accompany the songs with their drums and shakers.

My Shadow

Sometimes I think my shadow
Plays a funny game:
He is forever changing
While I remain the same.
In the early morning,
He's long as he can be,
Long and lean and lanky,
And twice as tall as me.
All morning, he keeps shrinking
'Til he is short and round.
At noon, he lies beneath my feet—
A puddle on the ground.
And then, he starts to stretch again,
Until by five or six,
He's lanky, lean, and long again.
I wish I knew his tricks.

Reproducible

Discussion

▶ What do you need to make a shadow? (A light source, a surface, and an opaque object between the light and the surface. The word *opaque* means light cannot go through and you cannot see through.)

▶ When is a shadow long? (When the light source is far away and low.)

▶ When is a shadow short? (When the light source is closer and overhead.)

▶ In the story of *Peter Pan* by J.M. Barrie (Puffin, 1996), Peter lost his shadow and Wendy had to sew it back on. Can that happen in real life? Why or why not?

Our Shadows

On a sunny day, take children outside to trace each others' shadows on large sheets of butcher paper. Do this as soon as they arrive, again at noon, and late in the afternoon. Label the shadow pictures with the time each was drawn. Post them with the caption "Our Shadows Shrink and Grow."

Alternative: If your children are experienced cutters, have them use their shadow pictures as patterns for cutting shadows from black butcher paper. Label and post the pictures on a bulletin board or classroom wall.

Shadow Experiments

In a darkened room, experiment with a flashlight and an opaque object, such as a ruler, cup, or glue bottle. How can you make the shadow long and thin? How can you make it short and wide?

Shadow Animals

In an otherwise dark room, have one source of light shining on the wall. With your hands, make shadow animals on the wall. Invite children to experiment to see what shapes they can make.

Me and My Shadow

Read the poem "My Shadow" by Robert Louis Stevenson found in *A Child's Garden of Verses* (Grosset & Dunlap, 1985). Ask children to compare Stevenson's poem to the one in this book. How are the two poems alike? How are they different? Which one do you like better? Why?

Shadow Puppets

Invite children to put on a shadow-puppet play. A very simple screen can be made by stretching white paper across a doorway, and fastening it with tape. A slide projector can be used for light. In this way, scenery can be projected on the screen. Caution your young puppeteers not to look at the projector light. The light source and puppets should be above the puppeteer's heads so their shadows do not show on the screen.

Puppets can be cut out of heavy dark cardboard. Attach a straw or pencil to the back of the puppet as a handle.

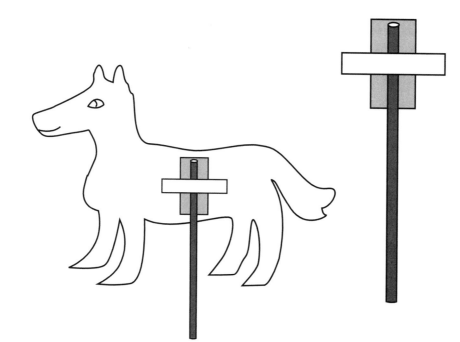

Shadow Tag

On a bright sunny day, let children play "Shadow Tag" outside. This is played like regular tag, except that the person who is "it" must step on another person's shadow instead of tagging the person.

Sun and Moon

The sun is most reliable–
He comes up every day.
Even when it's raining,
He doesn't go away;
But hides behind a cloud
Until the rain is done.
And then, he comes and shines for me,
My faithful friend, the sun.

The moon is quite another tale:
She can't decide if she
Is going to rise, and if she does,
What shape she's going to be.
Some nights, she'll be quite skinny:
And then she'll start to grow.
You'd think, when she was big and round,
She'd stay that way, but no!
She makes herself diminish
'Til she's hardly there at all.
I don't know why she wouldn't stay
A lovely golden ball.

The moon's forever playing tricks.
I think she likes to play.
But I prefer my faithful sun
Who comes to me each day.

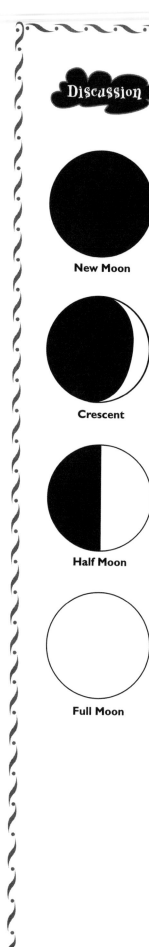

New Moon

Crescent

Half Moon

Full Moon

Discussion

▶ What does the word *reliable* mean? (dependable)

▶ Why did the child in the poem like the sun better than the moon? (He thought the sun was more reliable, more dependable.)

▶ What does *diminish* mean? (get smaller)

▶ He liked the moon best when it was full. When do you think the moon is most beautiful?

▶ Why does the sun come every day? (The earth keeps turning towards the sun as it makes its year-long trip around the sun. It makes a complete turn every twenty-four hours.)

▶ Why doesn't the moon appear every day? (While the earth is moving around the sun, the moon is moving around the earth. The rotation of the moon around the earth takes twenty-nine days.)

During part of these twenty-nine days, the moon is in the sky, but we can't see it. This happens when the sun, earth, and moon are lined up and the moon is in the middle. The moon has no light of its own, but shines in reflected sunlight. When the moon is in the middle, the sun is shining on the side of the moon we can't see. Our side is in a shadow. This dark moon is called a "New Moon" because it is considered to be the beginning of the moon's twenty-nine day cycle.)

▶ How does the moon appear to change shape? (The moon gradually moves to where the sun shines more and more on the side we see. After two or three days, we see a slender, curved part of it called a *crescent*, which grows into a stubby half pie at seven days.

At fourteen days, the moon is round and golden, a full moon. Then it gets smaller and smaller until it is dark again. Twenty-nine days have passed and the cycle begins again.)

48

Moon Phase Activity

Give children bright yellow construction paper and ask them to cut out pictures of their favorite moon phases. Use paper plates as patterns and mount the pictures on black construction paper. Label the moon phases in white crayon.

Comparison Poems

The poem, "Sun and Moon" is a comparison poem. Ask children to write their own poems comparing two items in nature, like valleys and mountains; water and land; and forests and deserts. Have children write their poems and draw the two items they compared.

What If?

Ask children, "What if you could travel to the sun or the moon? What do you think it would be like?" Ask them to draw a picture of themselves visiting the sun or moon.

Our Solar System

Explain to children that the sun and moon are part of our solar system. Our solar system includes the sun and everything that orbits the sun: Mercury, Venus, Earth, Mars, Jupiter, Saturn, Uranus, Neptune, and Pluto; the moons that orbit the planets; plus comets, asteroids, and meteoroids. Our solar system is part of a galaxy called the *Milky Way*.

Using reference books as guides, encourage children to work together to make models or drawings of the solar system. Teach children the names of the planets and their locations relative to the sun.

Moon Facts

Explain that Earth is not the only planet in our solar system with a moon. Mars has two moons, Jupiter has sixteen, Neptune has eight, and Pluto has one. Over 20 moons have been identified around Saturn and 15 are known to orbit Uranus.

Related Books for Young Children

What Makes Day and Night? by Franklyn M. Branley (Harper, 1980)

What the Moon Is Like by Franklyn M. Branley (Harper, 1986)

The Planets by Kate Petty (Watts, 1984)

The Sun: Our Nearest Star by Franklyn M. Branley (Harper, 1988)

Rabbit

A rabbit lives in my backyard.
I see him every day.
Sometimes he sits and looks at me;
I think he wants to play.
But when I move toward him,
He quickly runs away.

Reproducible

▶ Why is the rabbit timid? (It has many enemies and has to be ready to run from them because it cannot fight effectively.)

▶ Who or what are its enemies? (Dogs, cats, foxes, crows, hawks, and people.)

▶ Sometimes wild animals are so cute, we think they would make good pets. Is it ever all right to raise wild animals in our homes? (Only if they are orphaned or injured and you follow the guidance of someone who knows how to care for young wild animals. Baby animals that appear to be alone may not be orphans. The mother may be hiding nearby. Raising wild animals is very hard. The following people may be able to help: park rangers, conservation officers, science teachers, zoo keepers, or veterinarians.)

▶ Rabbits are one kind of mammal. *Mammals* are warm-blooded animals that feed their newborns mothers' milk. Mammals have backbones and almost all have hair or fur. *Warm-blooded* means that regardless of outside temperatures, the blood temperature remains the same. What other mammals can you name? (dogs, cats, hamsters, mice, horses, cows)

Field Trip

Take a field trip to a farm or zoo. Look for animals that are mammals. After returning to the classroom, discuss which animals you saw are mammals and which are not. List on the chalkboard all the animals you saw on the field trip. Encourage volunteers to come up to the board and sort the animals into mammals and those that are not. Challenge the children to list the characteristics that all mammals have in common.

Rabbit Ears

Give each child a two inch (5 cm) wide strip of construction paper, long enough to make a headband. Size the headband to fit around each child's head. Then tape the ends of the bands together. Help children cut out two six inch (15 cm) rabbit ears from pink or white construction paper. Glue the ears to the headband. As you read the poem, invite children to act out the part of the rabbit.

My Backyard

Have children think about the kinds of birds or animals that live in their backyards or in a nearby park. Ask them to draw an action picture of an animal doing something they've observed.

Caterpillar

Caterpillar, caterpillar,
Wiggle, wiggle, squirm,
Caterpillar, caterpillar,
You're a lowly worm.
Crawling on the ground,
Wiggling up a tree,
Who would ever guess
How lovely you will be.
When you've eaten all you need
And shed your wrinkled skin,
You will be a chrysalis
Waiting to begin—
Waiting to begin your life
As a butterfly,
Bringing beauty to my world
Until the day you die.
So fly, butterfly—
Fly, fly, fly!

Reproducible

▶ Why would the caterpillar want to climb up a tree? (probably to eat some leaves)

▶ How did the caterpillar become a chrysalis? (by shedding its skin. The caterpillar sheds its skin many times. When it eats, it becomes fatter and its skin becomes too tight. The skin then splits and the caterpillar wiggles out. There is a new skin underneath which hardens into a chrysalis, a shell-like body with no legs or head. Chrysalis can often be found hanging from branches or twigs.

▶ Why does the caterpillar become a chrysalis? (so it can grow wings and change into a butterfly inside the chrysalis)

▶ When the chrysalis breaks and the butterfly comes out, what does the butterfly do? (It flies around looking beautiful. The female butterfly lays eggs to make more caterpillars.)

Caterpillar

To make a caterpillar puppet, children will need:
- 12" (30 cm) chenille stems
- pencils, scissors, and tape
- 3" x 3" (7.5 cm x 7.5 cm) piece of light-weight cardboard
- pattern for 1½" (3.75 cm) circle
- black pen or fine-line marker

1. Have children fold the ends of the chenille stems twice so there are no sharp points. Show the children how to wrap the chenille stems around their pencils. Help children carefully remove the stems from the pencils and stretch them out if they are too tightly curled.

2. Have children trace a circle on cardboard. Invite them to draw a face on the circle and then cut it out. Tape the circle to one end of the chenille stem. Bend the other end of the stem to create a handle.

Butterfly Puppet

To make a butterfly puppet, children will need:

▶ round-wooden clothespins

▶ solid-colored paper napkin, luncheon size

▶ colored, gummed circles, various sizes from ¼ inch (approximately 1 cm) to 1¼ inches (approximately 3 cm)

▶ one yard (90 cm) of heavy, black thread (buttonhole thread)

▶ transparent tape (¾ inches wide) (approximately 1.75 cm)

1. Have each child tie one end of thread around the "neck" of his or her clothespin. Fold the napkin in half. Push the folded side of the napkin into the clothespin, until it looks like a butterfly's wings.

2. Invite children to decorate their butterflies with gummed circles. Have children tape the free end of the black thread to the body of the clothespin.

3. Encourage children to draw faces on the flat end of the clothespin. Have children place looped thread over their hands and tip from side to side to make their butterflies fly.

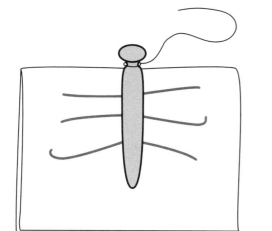
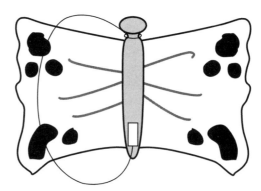

Act Out the Poem

After you and the children make the caterpillar and butterfly puppets, re-read the poem, "Caterpillar," to the class. As you read, mimic the actions of the caterpillar and the butterfly with your puppets. Have children copy your actions using their puppets.

At the beginning of the poem keep the butterfly puppet in one hand behind your back. When the caterpillar becomes a chrysalis, move the caterpillar puppet behind you out of sight. On the word "butterfly," have the butterfly puppet fly out from behind you.

Repeat the poem and have the children act out the poem with their puppets while you read.

To a Baby Frog

Little tadpole in my pond,
Wiggle, flip and swim.
See that big frog by the pond?
Some day you'll look like him.

Some day you will grow some legs
And, later, on, I hear,
You'll grow two lungs and lose your gills;
Your tail will disappear.

Like other tadpoles, you will be
A grown-up frog someday.
You cannot be a baby long,
For that is nature's way.

Discussion

▶ What does the poem say will happen to the tadpole? (He'll grow some legs, lose his gills, grow two lungs, and his tail will disappear.)

▶ Study these books to learn more about tadpoles and frogs.
Tadpole and Frog by Christine Back (Silver Burdett Press, 1986)
Discovering Frogs by Douglas Florian (Charles Scribner's Sons, 1986)

Nature Study

If possible, visit and revisit a pond to see tadpoles at various stages of development. Or, bring tadpoles, at intervals, into your room.

Tadpole Facts:

Share this information about tadpoles with the class.

▶ How did the tadpole get in the pond? (A female frog lays eggs in a pond and a male frog covers them with a liquid from his body so they can develop into tadpoles. The eggs are enclosed in jelly balls that stick together. After about ten days the tadpoles wiggle out.)

▶ What do tadpoles eat? (At first, tadpoles eat small plants. Later, when they are more developed, they eat insects.)

▶ Does the tadpole have any enemies? (Fish, birds, diving beetles, water scorpions, and pollution are its enemies. Tadpoles can escape from most of them by hiding under leaves and weeds, but pollution is hard to escape.)

▶ What is the tadpole's development schedule? (At five weeks, a tadpole grows back legs, and at six weeks, the nose and lungs appear. At ten weeks, it grows front legs and its eyes and mouth grow larger. Between thirteen and fifteen weeks, the tadpole crawls out of the pond and begins life as a frog, usually before its tail is completely absorbed into its body.)

Frog Puppet

To make a frog puppet, children will need:

- 5" x 5" (12.5 cm x 12.5 cm) square green construction paper
- 4" x 4" (10 cm x 10 cm) square pink construction paper
- black fine-line marker
- pencil, scissors, and glue
- coffee cup and smaller-size cup

Frog Puppet

1. Place a coffee cup on green construction paper. Trace around it and cut out the circle. This is the frog's head.

2. Place a smaller-size cup on pink construction paper. Trace around the cup and then cut out the construction-paper circle. This is the inside of the frog's mouth.

Frog Mouth

green —→
fold line —→
pink —→

3. Fold both circles in half. Match the fold lines of the two circles. Glue the pink circle to the inside of the green circle.

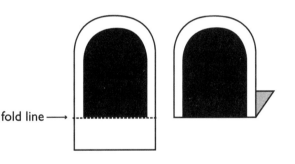

fold line —→

4. Make two eyes out of white construction-paper scraps. Use markers to color the center of the eyes. To make a three-dimensional eye, fold back the bottom of the eye just below the black center (see illustration). Repeat for the other eye. Glue the eye flaps to the top of the frog's head. Allow to dry before handling.

5. Cut four 1½" x ½" (3.75 cm x 1.25 cm) wide strips of green construction paper. Fold the strips accordion style. Have children glue the back legs to the bottom of the frog's head and front legs to the sides of the frog's head. Allow to dry before handling.

To operate the frog puppet, have each child place a thumb under the frog's head and a finger in back of each eye. Show the children how to press their fingers down to close the frog's mouth and release them to open it.

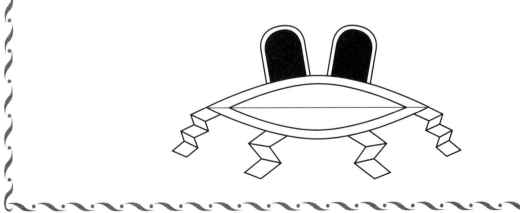

Vegetables

Corn is O.K.; asparagus is nice.
Carrots are tasty and peas will suffice.
But the vegetable that I like best,
Better than beets or all the rest,
Is firm and green and long and lean;
The delicious, nutritious green string bean.

Reproducible

Discussion

▶ What does the word *suffice* mean? (Okay; will do)

▶ What does the word *nutritious* mean? (providing food needed for health)

▶ What is your favorite vegetable? What do you like about it?

▶ What are some other foods which help us to be healthy? (Examples: grains, milk, fruit, fish, chicken)

▶ Why are these foods good for us? (vitamins, minerals, protein)

Raw Vegetable Salad

Have children bring in raw vegetables for a salad. Do not assign vegetables. Make the salad from whatever is contributed. After all the vegetables are cut and mixed together, serve as a snack on paper plates with a creamy dip.

Vegetable Prints

Make vegetable prints using carrots, celery stalks, and potatoes. Make a stamp pad by sprinkling powdered paint or by brushing tempera paint onto a wet folded paper towel in a shallow dish. Cut vegetables in half and press the flat surfaces into the stamp pad. Then press the paint-covered vegetables on paper. Allow prints to dry before handling.

Children can make designs or use prints as the basis of a picture, adding details with paintbrushes or crayons.

Vegetable Poem

Ask children to make up short poems about their favorite vegetables. Remind them to use words that describe the color, shape, and texture of the vegetables. Encourage each child to write his or her poem on writing paper and then illustrate it. Display the poems around the classroom.

Circle Time

Invite children to take turns substituting a child's name in the line "*Kesha, Kesha,* tell me true. How does your garden grow?" The child whose name is called should then respond by naming three vegetables that grow in his or her garden "all in a row."

Related Books for Young Children

Amanda and the Magic Garden by John Himmelman (Viking, 1987)
The Giant Vegetable Garden by Nadine Bernard Wescott (Little, Brown, 1981)

Dandelions

Mother says that dandelions
Are only common weeds.
She doesn't like their yellow blooms
Or like their flying seeds.

I think they're pretty flowers;
Their little golden heads
Look like drops of sunshine
On lawns and flower beds.

And when they're white and fuzzy,
I give a little puff,
And soon the air is bouncing
With dandelion fluff.

They look like little parachutes
Floating in the breeze.
I'm glad that there are plenty
Of flowers such as these.

Reproducible

Discussion

> What is the difference between a weed and a flower? (A weed is a plant or flower growing where it is not wanted.)

> Why did Mother think the dandelions were weeds? (She didn't want them in her lawn choking some of the grass.)

> Why did the child ("I" in the poem) like dandelions? (They are pretty. It's fun to blow the seeds.)

> What are some flowers often considered weeds? (Queen Anne's Lace, Daisies, Chicory, Clover, Indian Paint Brush, Vetch)

Nature Study

If you know of an available meadow or empty lot, ask the owner's permission to take the children to see and possibly pick the weed flowers. Before the fieldtrip, check with the Environmental Protection Agency or your County Extension office to be sure none of the flowers are protected against picking. It is also important to find out ahead of time if any children are allergic to certain plants, such as ragweed or goldenrod. Take along several flower and wild flower reference books to help children identify wild flowers and weeds.

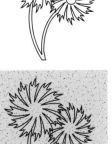

Spatter Painting with Weed Flowers

Place paper on a work surface covered with newspaper. Fill a window spray-cleaner bottle with thin paint. Have children place flowers face down on the paper and spray around them. Allow the pictures to dry before removing flowers. Children can repeat with other flowers and other colors.

Flower Collage

Have children cut out pictures of flowers from old magazines or seed catalogues. Encourage children to glue the pictures on construction paper to make a flower collage or a flower garden.

Paper Plate Flower Garden

Invite children to make dandelions, daisies and other types of flowers from paper plates, yarn and green construction paper. Have each child color or paint one side of a paper plate. Encourage them to glue yarn around the edges to give the flowers a three-dimensional look. Have them cut stems and leaves from green construction paper and attach with glue or tape. Ask children to write their names on the flower stems. Display the flowers in a class garden on your wall or bulletin board.

Rub-A-Dub-Dub,
That's Me in the Tub

Today, I played at "Hide and Seek,"
Beneath the trees, beside the creek.

Of course, I got a little dirt
Upon myself, upon my shirt.

My mom insists a bath's a must
To rid myself of grime and dust.

Each reminder of the day,
Of exciting times at play,
Must be rubbed and washed away.

Mom will scrub each foot and knee
'Til I don't even look like me!

Reproducible

- Is it possible to play or work outside without getting at least a little bit dirty?

- What are the two kinds of dirt mentioned in the poem? (dust—dry powdery dirt; and grime—ground in dirt)

- What are some names for outdoor dirt? (earth, soil, sand, clay)

- What do we call wet dirt? (mud)

- Dirt can be a problem, but it is also useful. How? (Dirt is necessary for growing grass, trees, vegetables, flowers and other plants. In hot, dry climates, people have made bricks called "adobe" from mud. A special kind of mud called "clay" is used to make vases, dishes, tiles and bricks.)

Clay Art

Buy clay from an art store. Invite children to make small figures by pinching the clay together. Give each child a ball of clay and have them squeeze the clay to remove any bubbles before shaping. Use water to thin down some of the clay until it is liquid. After the children have finished molding their figures have them smooth liquid clay over the outside of them before drying. This will give the clay figures a smoother surface. If you do not have access to a pottery kiln, small figures can be dried in the sun over a period of time.

Fun with Mud

How much water does it take to turn dirt into mud? If you have the facilities and don't mind the mess, let children experiment to find out. This would be a good outside project with a small group. (Have plenty of paper towels handy for cleanup.) Give each child or group of children a cottage-cheese bucket half filled with dirt. Have them add small amounts of water to the dirt and stir it with craft sticks until they have mud.

If the mud is not too watery, it can be used like clay to make figures or mud pies. Children can make mud handprints on paper or write their names in mud using their fingers.

Mud

Read the book *MUD* by Wendy Cheyette Lewison (Random House, 1990) to the class. When you finish reading, ask children if they would like to be the boy or girl in the book. Why or why not? Also ask them why they think children like mud more than adults.